WHAM'S LAST STAND!

● *Photographer MURRAY SANDERS (25) finds a provincial, national and international market for his pictures from his home in Portsmouth. He specialises in sport, pop and feature material.*

● *Thanks to photo-technicians Keith Tuttle and Steve Whale and to Alan and Kirsty at Ocean Photographics, Southsea, Portsmouth.*

WHAM'S LAST STAND!

Photographs by Murray Sanders

Text by John Travis

SIDGWICK & JACKSON
LONDON

First published in Great Britain in 1986
by Sidgwick and Jackson Limited
1 Tavistock Chambers, Bloomsbury Way,
London WC1A 2SG

Photographs copyright © Murray Sanders

Text copyright © Sidgwick and Jackson

Designed by Steve Cray, paste-up by Jim Tomlin.

ISBN 0-283-99438-X

Phototypeset by Portsmouth & Sunderland Newspapers plc.
The News Centre, Hilsea, Portsmouth.

Printed in Great Britain by Blantyre Printing Limited.

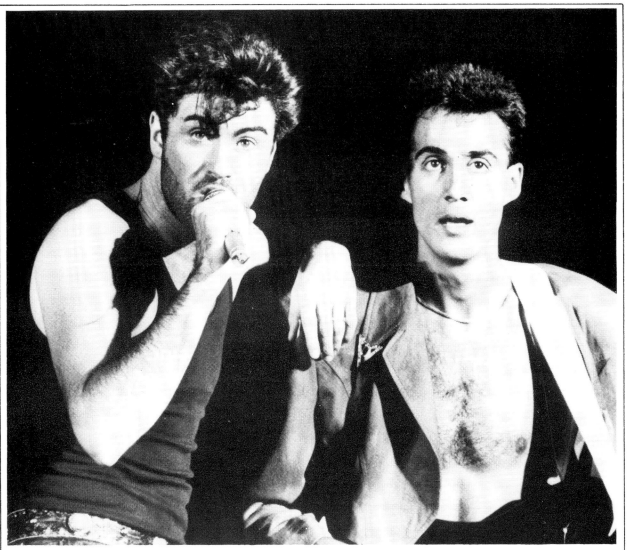

● *Young heartbreakers!*

TEARS AND CHEERS . . .end of the road for Wham! who dominated the Eighties pop scene.

Wham! The Final. Saturday 28 June 1986; seventy-two thousand fans packed into Wembley Stadium, most of them heart-broken because it was the end of the road for a duo that had dominated the early Eighties. The end of an era for George Michael and Andrew Ridgeley.

The pair had gone a long way in the four years they had been together. Their infectious pop tunes and their dynamic good looks had touched the hearts of millions.

But they quit while they were ahead. The hits, the videos, and the memories will live on, and when time looks back on Wham!'s place in pop history it will surely see them where they belong, among the all-time greats.

George provided a unique song-writing expertise. Andrew provided the carefree self-confidence that appealed to the fans, who craved to be like them. George began impossibly shy, Andrew was never afraid to do anything. But only together did the songs and the image gel. They were a perfect complement for each other.

Looking back, the story

WHAM! ALBUMS: Aug 83 **Fantastic** — Bad Boys / A Ray Of Sunshine/Love Machine/Wham Rap/Club Tropicana/Nothing Looks The Same In The Light / Come On! / Young Guns (Got For It); Nov 84 **Make It Big** — Wake Me Up Before You Go Go / Everything She Wants / Heartbeat / Like A Baby / Freedom / If You Were There / Credit Card Baby / Careless Whisper; Jul 86 **The Final** — Wham Rap / Young Guns / Bad Boys / Club Tropicana / Wake Me Up Before You Go Go / Careless Whisper / Freedom / Last Christmas / Everything She Wants / I'm Your Man / Blue (Armed With Love) / A Different Corner / Battlestations / Where Did Your Heart Go / The Edge Of Heaven.

TEAMWOR

S PURE . . . .

WHAM! SINGLES: Oct 82 Young Guns (Go For It) / Going For It; Jan 83 Wham! Rap / Wham! Rap Club Mix; May 83 Bad Boys / Instrumental; Jul 83 Club Tropicana Blue (Armed With Love); Dec 83 Club Fantastic Megamix — A Ray Of Sunshine/Come On!/Love Machine; May 84 Wake Me Up Before You Go Go / Instrumental; Oct 84 Freedom / Instrumental; Dec 84 Last Christmas / Everything She Wants; Nov 85 I'm Your Man / Do It Right; Jun 86 The Edge Of Heaven / Where Did Your Heart Go / Battlestations / Wham! Rap '86; **George Michael Singles:** Aug 86 Careless Whisper / Instrumental; Apr 86 A Different Corner / Instrumental.

reads like a fairy-tale, but it happened nevertheless. Two boys emerged from suburbia to captivate the world. Remember the immortal words of George and Andy — 'Go For It'.

At 2 p.m. the crowds burst into Wembley Stadium. Scores had been waiting outside overnight to get the best positions. The terraces and turf filled with Wham!'s peers from the suburbs. Soul boys, showing they possessed as much dress sense as George and Andrew. Girls, excitable, excited, desperate for their last glimpse. A smattering of mums and dads, pretending they were only there as chaperons. And an entire private enclosure of friends, family, and celebrities.

George arrived at the stadium in a black Daimler limousine with girlfriend, Kathy Jueng. Before the gates opened he ventured on to the stage to savour some of the atmosphere before it erupted in a few hours' time.

Andrew arrived about an hour later than George, in another limousine with his girlfriend, model Donya Fiorentino.

The backstage area should have been christened 'Club Tropicana'. Elton John had flamboyantly installed a 15-foot-long swimming-pool next to his dressing-room, at a cost of £15,000. The pool was irresistible on that hot summer's day, and stars and guests took the plunge to cool their bodies and release tension. Around the pool were video screens,

keeping everyone aware of what was going on on stage.

The gathering crowd were kept amused first by Gary Glitter. Nothing serious in music or style, Gary was there just for fun, leaping around despite his now bulky frame, remembering his own days of glory in the early Seventies.

Then Nick Heyward, whose days with Haircut 100 coincided with the start of George and Andrew's career. He, too, reminded the audience of his most successful moments with 'Love Plus One' and 'Fantastic Day' mixed in with his newer solo material.

The afternoon lingered on. Little ripples of restlessness went around the stadium. Time to make yourself comfortable for the onslaught. The stage was being prepared. Then suddenly the giant video screens on either side of the stage lit up. It was the premier of the film *Wham! In China — Foreign Skies.*

The crowd responded almost as if the real concert had begun, screaming as their idols spoke on screen or gyrated in front of the bemused Chinese audience. No one seemed to mind that the songs they were hearing would be repeated live within the next few hours. They relished every moment. The atmosphere was reaching fever pitch, especially when Andrew and George filled the entire 30-foot-high screens.

The video screens fall dark and silent. THE FINAL appears in giant letters on a stage set resembling the sails of a Chinese

junk. An excited buzz hovers over the stadium. The crowd shouts 'We want Wham!'. At 7.40 p.m. the shout turns into a triumphant roar as the first beats of 'Everything She Wants' sound from behind the curtain. Seventy-two thousand pairs of lungs and feet resound together.

The curtain draws back and George appears on stage, his hair clipped short, dressed in a black, body-hugging vest, tight trousers, and fringed leather jacket. He moves like a street warrior. Flanked by two male dancers who silhouette his moves, he snakes his way up and down both catwalks, protruding tantalizingly into the crowd.

Another roar goes up when Andrew makes his grand entrance. He is wedged between the glamorous Whamettes, Shirlie Holliman and Pepsi Demacque. Andrew wants to be erotic. He peels off a black leather glove and throws it into the audience. They surge for it like bees around a honey-pot. The spotlights go up, a guitar is handed to Andrew, and 'Everything She Wants' bursts into life.

It is followed by 'Club Tropicana', heralding a frenzied burst of audience activity — being squeezed together does not cramp their enthusiasm. Those at the front who might be getting too hot and dry are sprayed with hose-pipes by the stage crew. Andrew stikes some guitar poses, George runs across the stage and slips his jacket off to expose his bare shoulders. He goes down on his knees, thrusting his pelvis forward.

'This is obviously the most important gig we have ever played,' George tells them. 'I think that in front of me is the best thing I have ever looked at.'

By now the audience is firmly under Wham!'s spell as they follow up with the infectious 'Heartbeat' from their second album. Then George asks: 'Do you feel like being sexy?' The answer can only be yes, It is time for the barnstorming 'Bad Boys'. Most of the attention is on George as his voice and movements captivate the stadium. But Andrew is not to be outdone and follows George by going out to the catwalk. He also gets a wild reaction.

The identity of the next performer is hardly a well kept secret when stage-hands wheel on a white grand piano. Elton John has become one of George's greatest admirers and personal friends. He springs on staged dressed as outrageously as ever in a Ronald McDonald clown outfit. He is content to play the role of accompanist on 'Edge Of Heaven', while George proves himself one of the few pop performers able to manipulate the huge Wembley crowd so proficiently. He splits them into three sections to help with the chorus, all competing against each other to please him best.

Just as the pace is taken to the brink, George decides to mellow out. He introduces a song he busked

Young Guns . . .

. . . go great guns!!

Wake Me Up Before You Go Go

You put the boom boom into my heart . . .

with his friend David Austin at Leicester Square tube station seven years before, 'Candle In The Wind'. It is a towering, emotive version, worthy of the master at the piano next to him himself. George is showing his real talent without the razzmatazz. Elton nods his head at the end in approval, and appears to say: 'I loved that.' They hug, and Elton is gone to thunderous appreciation.

'Credit Card Baby' gets everyone going again. George remarks: 'This is definitely a horny crowd.' Carly Simon's classic 'Why?' get's the Wham! interpretation next. It is a bitter-sweet song, chosen perfectly for the occasion.

'I know it's not the right time of year,' George tells the crowd, 'But just imagine it's winter time.' With that he goes into 'Last Christmas', provoking an impromptu chorus from 72,000 backing singers. Pleased with his massed choir, George tests the audience to see if it can look as good as it sounds. The concert programmes are printed with one cover in orange and the other in blue. George tells them he wants to see The Wave. 'If you have a programme please lift up the orange part of your programme.' An orange wave ripples around the stadium. George loves the effect. He then repeats it with a sea of blue. 'That's brilliant,' he says. 'That looks fantastic.'

Time for more nostalgia. 'We are going to go a long way back, as far back as

you can possibly go in the Wham! story. This next song was composed in Andrew's front room. It was the first record we ever made.' 'Wham! Rap'.

George tantalizingly introduces 'A Different Corner' next. 'I'd like to dedicate this to someone special,' he says. 'She knows who she is.' After it is over he wipes away a tear. He has always been secretive about his love affairs.

Wembley erupts after 'Freedom' as George and Andrew leave the stage.

They get a standing ovation, but everyone knows this is not quite the end. George returns for 'Careless Whisper'. Would they have been so good together, could they have lasted forever? Maybe George is singing it to Andy. It is one of the emotional high points — there must be plenty of mascara-stained tears and manly lumps in the throat.

The hush is halted by the return of Andrew, Shirlie, and Pepsi, blazing 'Young Guns', followed by 'Wake Me Up Before You Go Go, I'm not planning on going solo'. Vaguely apt lyrics, and one of their personal favourites. More than two hours of exhausting performance, and still George bounds from one side of the stage to the other, posing provocatively on the catwalk, sending gasps and murmurs through the female ranks.

Again Wham! try to take their final bow. Yet again they are brought back, but now it really is the end with 'I'm Your Man'. However the surprises, or 'more goals' that George had promised earlier, are not quite over. Simon Le Bon, who has been backstage with his wife Yasmin, joins them.

George sinks his head on to Andy's shoulder, turns to the crowd, and says goodbye. He does not linger long. It is as if the moment is all too much for him. The same goes for Andrew. They slope off stage to another thunderous ovation. Within moments the night sky is illuminated with £60,000-worth of fireworks. Rockets erupt overhead and The Final concert is over.

The night is not quite over, though. For Wham! are holding an exclusive party. They spend an estimated £50,000 taking over the Hippodrome disco on its busiest night of the week. Traffic is at a standstill outside the club and barriers are erected on the four corners that lead into Leicester Square. Inside, the Hippodrome has been specially redecorated with swathes of silk hanging from the ceilings and walls. An hour-and-a-half after the concert George and Andy turn up in the limousines. They don't leave until 4 a.m.

The Split

It was the hardest decision Wham! ever had to make and it is doubtful whether George and Andrew will ever have to make a more important career decision. But not everyone realizes, even today, that the decision to call it a day was taken several months before it was made public.

When the news broke on 22 February 1986 the fans were shocked. How could they do it? Had their two idols had a huge row? Why quit when they had so much to offer and when things were going so well? What will they do next? Questions no one thought they would have to ask for many years.

The decision was taken the previous summer, at the time 'I'm Your Man' was

written. George summed up the reasons: 'We'd done everything that we set out to do, since we first thought of going into music at school. We were right at the top. I think eventually I'll look back and say that these were probably the most exciting two years I've ever had. But to go on like this would drive me absolutely crazy. I'm getting older, you know, so I've got to replace it with something more valid to the

way I feel. Having said that, I wouldn't take back any of the last two years, Apart from some of the videos and haircuts I don't think I've made any wrong moves.'

The first the fans knew about the split was when they picked up their morning newspapers. The headlines were enough to make them choke on their cornflakes. George had issued an official statement saying he had decided to

leave his management company Nomis, and that he was planning to release a solo LP. The statement was put out hastily because George wanted to distance himself from plans to sell Nomis to a leisure company with strong South African ties. (As a result of the Wham! split the deal fell through).

But the fans were not the only people shocked at George's statement. At the time Andrew was relaxing in his new apartment in the tax haven of Monte Carlo. Why had Andrew not been told before George made the official announcement? 'This was a personal decision on my part,' was George's explanation. 'I was not able to discuss the position with Andrew because he has been out of contact in France.'

The fans were distraught. Within hours of the split becoming public they besieged the Wham! office and record company with phone calls and letters. The reaction was a tribute to how much the duo had touched so many people, but it was futile — the decision was final. At least Wham! were to go out in spectacular fashion with a farewell concert at Wembley Stadium that sold out within hours of the tickets going on sale.

The Future

George and Andrew will doubtless remain friends, but the future will see them taking different paths. As George forges ahead with his musi-

cal career, Andrew will broaden his horizons into acting and motor racing.

Speculation that George will form a new group with his friend for the past ten years, David Austin, is unfounded. George may act as a producer for David, he may write a couple of tracks for an LP, and even sing on it, but the liaison is likely to

end there. It is doubtful George will want to tie himself down to another group. He is set to release his debut solo album before Christmas 1986, which no doubt will enhance the reputation that began with the singles 'Careless Whisper' and 'A Different Corner'. He will concentrate on his song writing and surely establish himself as one of the great song writers of the day.

In the meantime he is also starting to fulfil some of his pesonal ambitions to work with great American stars. He has already recorded songs with Aretha Franklin, and given the chance would like to get together with Michael Jackson and Stevie Wonder.

Whether we see George the live performer again is open to question. There is no doubting his phenomenal stage presence, but the fact is he prefers working behind the scenes. Live appearances are likely to be at a premium, but when they happen they promise to be worth waiting for.

Now that Andrew has acquired enormous personal wealth from the Wham! partnership, he is free to do whatever he wishes. It is unlikely that music will be uppermost in his thoughts, at least for the time being. His fascination with motor racing is showing no sign of waning, despite Renault pulling out from sponsoring him. He has sufficient personal funds to cover that set back and will want to give himself more time to get established in the sport.

Andrew's love affair with

SHADY . . . Cool Andrew bows out in style!

pop has long since worn off. If he ever decides to get involved in music again, George may be the first one to help with any production. But what Andrew said recently is likely to prove significant. 'George has the greater talent so it's going to overshadow mine. I can sing a bit but not as well as him so what's the point.'

Many people, including Simon Napier-Bell, think that Andrew's real future could lie on the screen. He has expressed considerable interest in film work. 'I'm waiting for the right script to come along,' he says. 'I've looked at quite a few but none have been quite what I am looking for.'

Will Wham! ever re-form is a question that no one knows the answer to. After such an emotional farewell it would be somewhat of an anticlimax were they to get back together. But such an event, especially in the form of a one-off, can never be ruled out. Certainly the fans would welcome it. Whether it would do George and Andrew's credibility any good is something else. Wham! were always about youth and exuberance. They were not around for very long, but it was great while it lasted. Perhaps it is best to remember them for what they were. Wembley Stadium was a great way to go. It would be hard to repeat it.

Heading East

In the summer of 1985 Wham! became the first major Western pop group to play China. They wanted to open new doors in a country that has been loathe to show itself to the outside world. In the end it did little but give a few thousand Chinese a glimpse of another way of life. The trip cost Wham! an estimated £1 million. But they did achieve one aim, to get instant world-wide publicity.

'If we knew what it was going to be like we would have thought twice about going. The Chinese Government used us as pawns to better their own ends,' says George.

At the Peking concert the crowd of 10,000 were warmed up by a DJ. To George, looking out from the wings, everything seemed normal — excitable girls were screaming with anticipation. But what he was not aware of was a

message that went out through the loudspeakers urging the fans to refrain from dancing during Wham!'s concerts, and to stay in their seats.

George and Andrew tried to incite the Peking audience into letting themselves go, but were greeted only with polite handclapping and the waving of a few scarves. When a few people did get carried away and attempted to stand up and dance they were ushered back to their seats by the Chinese police, and some were even arrested. The Chinese officials sitting in the front rows seemed delighted, but the band felt cheated.

'There was a huge cultural difference which there is no way to cross in an hour and a half,' recalls George. 'It was frustrating to have dignitaries sitting in front, and the younger Chinese were intimidated by the police.'

It seems that Wham!'s brave attempt to bridge the cultural divide had little chance of success. But their pioneering efforts are likely to be recognized as a landmark in opening up Western popular culture to the East.

They stayed on in Peking for an interview while the rest of the party took a plane to Canton. Thousands of feet in the air 30-year-old Portuguese trumpeter, Raul de Oliveira, went berserk. He grabbed a penknife, ran down the aisle, and began stabbing himself in the stomach. Still in a frenzy he careered into the cockpit. The pilot temporarily lost control and the plane dipped several thousand

feet. Security guards managed to catch him and the plane returned to Peking, where de Oliveira was given treatment in a mental hospital.

It's A Deal

Dreams of becoming an overnight sensation crashed when their first single 'Wham! Rap', flopped. Then came 'Young Guns', their personal anthem. It crawled up the charts, finally reaching the Top 30 and with it the offer of an appearance on *Top of the Pops*. This time it looked like they were there. 'Young Guns' reached Number Three in October 1982.

'Wham! Rap' was re-released and reached Number Eight at the start of 1983. They looked unstoppable when their third single, 'Bad Boys', peaked at Number Two. At the same time they toughened up their image with macho black leather and a £10,000 video, based on *West Side Story*.

The hits were rolling in, but wealth was eluding them. They were offered a better deal by Simon Napier-Bell, who said he would make them a worldwide success, and millionaires. Napier-Bell

FULL STRETCH

George puts his back into it . . . to delight thousands of devoted fans.

was an old hand in the music industry having managed The Yardbirds in the sixties, Marc Bolan in the seventies, and, more recently, Japan. He set about freeing George and Andrew from their Innervision deal. But for the moment the show carried on. A tour was organized to promote Wham!'s debut album *Fantastic*, which went straight to Number One. Their sexy, carefree image and infectious pop tunes were irresistible.

Women

George is a man of mystery as far as romantic inclinations are concerned. He has not had many well-publicized romances, in spite of the romantic tenor of his talent.

Andrew, however, has always been the man who lives for the moment. His romantic exploits must be the envy of many of his peers. He has always been good looking and admits; 'It's physically fulfilling sleeping with a lot of girls.' He adds, however, 'But I know we miss out emotionally.'

One of Andrew's first serious relationships was with Wham! backing singer, Shirlie Holliman. But he soon lost her to Spandau Ballet's Martin Kemp, and the couple have since married. There then followed a series of glamorous, short-lived liaisons. He said: 'I'm infatuated with women. I absolutely adore women. It may be the young buck phase, but so what. I have no intention of cooling down.'

In recent months Andrew seems to have settled down with 18-year-old American model, Donya Fiorentino, who previously went out with Don Johnson.

George, in comparison, suffered from being the Adrian Mole of his class. As a youngster the ugly duckling was overweight, wore thick glasses, and had unkempt hair. However, this phase did not last long, and soon he found himself one of the most eligible sex symbols of the decade. But he still seemed to be the most serious partner of Wham! both professionally and romantically. His name has been linked with his personal assistant, Pat Fernandez, but this could be just press gossip. At the farewell concert he was in the company of beautiful American oriental Kathy Jueng.

Marriage for George seems out of the question in the near future — he is reported to have said he would favour marriage in his late twenties. If and when it does happen, it will blight the lives of the thousands of girls who hold him close to their hearts.

Quids In!

The legal moves to extricate Wham! from Innervision were already in motion by the time 'Club Tropicana' was a hit in the summer of 1983. The song was inspired by soul-boy haunt, the Beat Route club in Soho. The protracted negotiations dragged on into the winter, however and halted the group's career. When an agreement was reached they were left with little money, but a promising new deal with the mighty CBS Records. As a parting shot, Innervision released 'Club Fantastic

Megamix', a three-track EP. It was immediately condemned by George and Andrew, who urged fans not to buy it. The record peaked at Number Fifteen, lower than their previous hits.

They had to wait for spring 1984 before releasing their next song, 'Wake Me Up Before You Go Go', the first on their new label. 'The perfect pop song', as George later described 'Go Go', became their first chart topper. That summer turned into a battle for hit song supremacy with Frankie Goes to Hollywood, whose 'Two Tribes' displaced Wham! from the top. George hit back in August with his solo 'Careless Whisper'. Rumours of a split were quickly scotched by George. 'Andrew plays guitar, is half the image, co-wrote 'Careless Whisper' with me, and if it wasn't for him, Wham! songs wouldn't be what they are. Wham! is an equal democratic partnership and it's going to stay that way,' was his reply.

Two months after 'Careless Whisper', 'Freedom' reached Number One, confirming Wham!'s superstar status. George's next appearance in the Number One slot was as part of Band Aid's 'Do They Know It's Christmas'. Ironically, it stopped Wham! themselves topping the charts with 'Last Christmas'. Inspired by Band Aid they donated the £250,000 royalties from 'Last Christmas' to the African Famine Appeal.

By the end of 1984 Wham! had sold over three million singles. Their second album, *Make It Big,* topped

the charts. And the former dole-queue boys were given the British Record Industry award for Best Group of the Year. Now they were starting to earn real money. They were due a break, but pushed themselves instead on to bigger and more ambitious challenges, with a world tour taking in Australia and the Far East.

Growing Up

Yorgus Kyriakou Panayatiou, Yog to his friends, was born on 25 June 1963.

George Michael's name was not quite so easy to remember in its original Greek Cypriot form. His parents, Jack and Lesley, lived in Finchley, North London, and brought him up in a close-knit atmosphere with sisters Melanie and Yioda.

Six months earlier, on 26 January, 1963, Andrew John Ridgeley was born in Windlesham Maternity Home, in the Berkshire countryside just outside London. The son of an Egyptian father, Albert Mario, and mother Jenny,

● *CARELESS WHISPER . . . Guilty feet have got no rhythm.*

● *ONE, TWO, THREE,*

LL TOGETHER NOW!

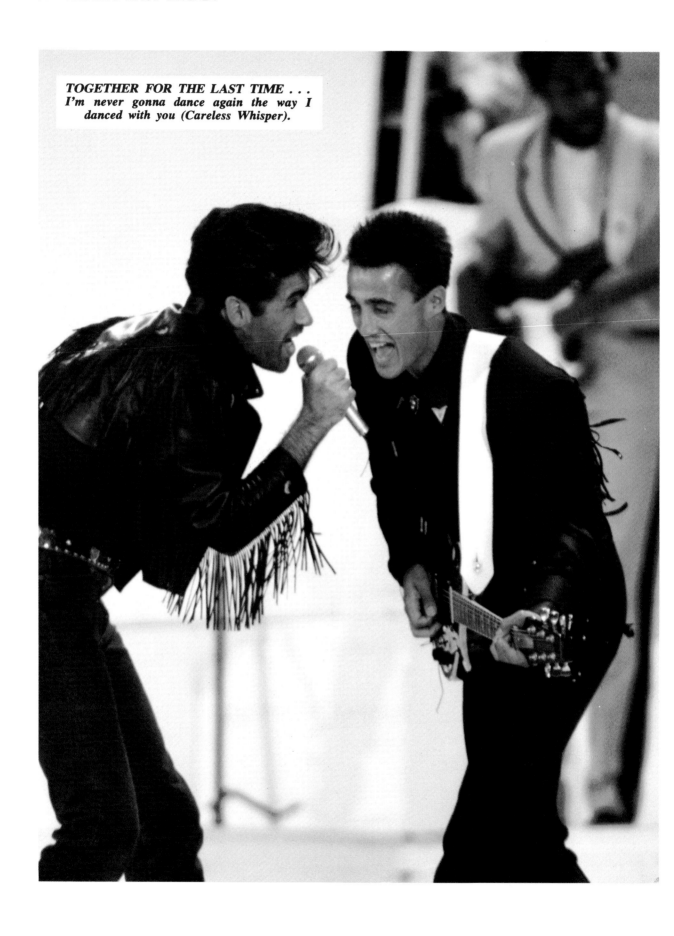

TOGETHER FOR THE LAST TIME . . .
I'm never gonna dance again the way I danced with you (Careless Whisper).

GEORGE MICHAEL . . . on the "Edge of Heaven".

he has one brother called Paul.

Andrew was by far the more outgoing and precocious child, but George was not above getting into mischief. He was caught stealing when he was nine-years-old, and later appreciated getting a good spanking. 'I remembered that humiliation and it probably stopped me somewhere along the line.' The combination of discipline and love and affection gave George a wide emotional experience. It is one of the reasons he can put so much feeling into many of his songs. Also he was still at home during his rise to fame. At an age when most young people distance themselves from their families, he was spending thousands of pounds keeping them by his side. The most extravagant example of this was when he took everyone with him to China.

George's first public singing appearance was in front of a neighbour. Early in the morning, still dressed in pyjamas, he used to go out by himself to collect bugs and insects. To keep himself company he sang out loud, and the neighbour reported back to his family what a good voice he had.

Andrew's habit of crashing racing cars has its roots in his childhood love of football and other outdoor activities. His injuries include two broken noses, a broken arm, a broken foot, and a dislocated knee. He suffered from a sweet tooth, too, on one occasion enduring twelve fillings in one session at the dentist. Andrew was also prone to being spanked a lot, mostly at school rather than home. On one school trip he got involved in a talcum powder fight and was desperately trying to clear up when the teacher walked in and dealt with him.

IT'S SIMPLE . . . Simon Le Bon joins in!

COOL BOY ...
George strips off as temperatures in the audience rise!

THAT'S OUR BOY . . .

It's a flag day for one young fan!

GOOD LUCK BOYS . . . from mascot Snoopy!

THE FINAL FAREWELL
... from thousands of adoring fans

Like A Baby

Say goodbye and don't tell me why you have to go . . . Wham! left Wembley with fans asking whether they'd ever see the million sellers play together again.

IT'S YOUR TURN . . . the Wembley audience get a last chance to join in with their idols.

HERE'S TO THE FUTURE ... *Andrew raises his glasses to the years to come!*

Reach for the sky . . .

★ **THE SKY'S THE LIMIT** for George Michael who says he'll stay in the pop business. He wants to go on to work with some of the great names of pop, including Michael Jackson, Stevie Wonder and Aretha Franklin.

LOOK NO HANDS . . . *this pop game's a piece of cake!*

It's that magic touch . . .

Cuddle up baby move in tight, we'll go dancing tomorrow night . . . sexy George drives 'em wild at Wembley.

RED HOT! Elton John joins the farewell to Wham!

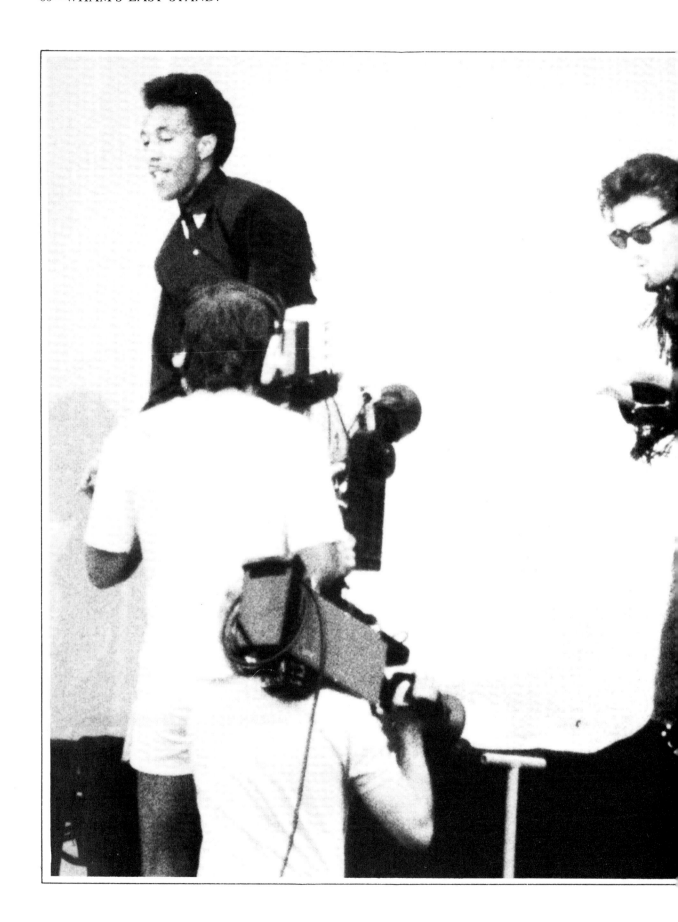

A PICTURE OF SUCCESS . . . George plays to the cameras.